Gold in Autumn

by

Karen Warinsky

To those who've been kind.

Acknowledgements

The author wishes to acknowledge the editors of the following publications and online sites in which these poems appeared, some in slightly different versions;

Mizmor 2019 Anthology, "Breaking the Firmament" and "Thoreau's Window;" a huge thank you to *The Montreal International Poetry Prize, 2011 Longlist Anthology*, "Roodhouse," and *The Montreal International Poetry Prize 2013 Global Poetry Anthology*, "Legacy;" *Light, a Journal of Photography and Poetry,* "Iron and Dust," and "Spanish Town;" Fried Chicken and Coffee.com, "Tough Girls" and "Some Nights;" *Deep Wild Journal,* "Spoken Word;" *Joy Interrupted, an anthology on motherhood and loss*; "The Wheel has Turned;" *Blue Heron Review*, "Lawn Chair."

Published by Human Error Publishing
Paul Richmond
www.humanerrorpublishing.com
paul@humanerrorpublishing.com

Copyright © 2020
by
Human Error Publishing & Karen Warinsky

All Rights Reserved

ISBN: 978-1-948521-40-6

Illustrations and cover art by Karen Warinsky
& Human Error Publishing

Human Error Publishing asks that no part of this publication be reproduced or transmitted in any form or by any means electronic or mechanical, including photocopy, recording or information storage or retrieval system without permission in writing from Karen Warinsky and Human Error Publishing. We ask that you do this to support us and the artist.

CONTENTS

Seeing Autumn	10
The Messenger	11
Tulips	12
Cold Stone	13
Stand and Sing	14
Asking the Question	16
My Friendly Neighborhood Nazi	17
Thoreau's Window	19
Breaking the Firmament	20
All the Useless Things	21
Arms around Mother Nature	22
Bus Ride	23
Down in Dublin	24
Words of the Masters	25
Christos	26
Hungry	27
Stars	28
Planets	30
Roseland Park	31
Legacy	32
Roman Ruin	33
The Eye	34
Spanish Town	35
Montecatini	36
Grecian Dream	37
Iron and Dust	38
The Great Divide	39
Crepe Paper Proms	41
Tough Girls	42
Some Nights	43
Down Home	44
Roodhouse	45
Cornfields	47
Saturday Night at the Shamrock	49
Asleep in the Field	51
Spoken Word	52
Portrait	53

What Summer Was	54
Pulling Rank	55
Light Bearers	56
Older	57
Dark Color	58
The Wheel has Turned	59
Superposition	61
The Evidence	62
Not Alice	63
Checked Out	64
Facing Grain	65
Birds Fallen	66
Archelogy	67
We Have Become Something	68
The Middle	69
Paper Bag	71
Process Processing	72
Gas Pump	73
Unexpected Friend	74
Cardinal Point	75
End of the World	76
Lawn Chair	77
The Apple	78
Living Out Loud	80
Phone Call	81
Blue Coat	82
Emily	83
The Circus	84
Last Autumn	85
Golden Cloud	86
Sunflower	87
Wiser	88

Seeing Autumn

Incandescent, gold and red,
the world vibrates and hums
with the last of the autumn.
Carmel and rust,
sable, tan and chocolate leaves ornament the ground,
while necklaces of green and gold
twist down off the sturdy trees.
Those trees will wait through another winter
before receiving spring's crown again.

Colors and sounds blurred in my hurried life
now demanding, insistent.
Burgundy tangles top the bushes,
while spear points turn to a pale gold, then white;
tasseled heads that greet and satisfy.

There is sweetness in the decay,
not repellent, but comforting.

How strange to walk through so much beauty
 and so much death
all at once.

So many daily petty troubles, missteps, and lost chances
are confronted in the face of this beauty, this ruin.
But there remains no answer.

Compelled as others before me,
 I sit and try to let in a piece to solve
this oldest puzzle of the world,
here in this autumn afternoon,
as all nature sheds its glory,
preparing for starker days, darker nights.

The Messenger

It is 3 o'clock and the afternoon traffic
flows, jolts, halts, then goes,
people heading to haircuts, appointments,
coffee breaks, home.

He stands at the intersection across from the gas station,
knit cap and heavy jacket secured to his body,
fitting tight, like an ideology.

A circle, a triangle, a rhomboid of the air,
he gestures,
sings a bit,
bores his bug eyes through the drivers
and their timid passengers,
relaying his message.

He shouts--
warns of things already known;
the state of the air, the ocean, the government,
dogs in Yulin, orphans in the Sudan,
refugees roaming the world.
He calls out in anguish of other news too,
things no one can prove, things most haven't heard.
His animation, his 3-D-ness compel us all to look,
if only for those few seconds before the car can turn,
head up the hill
and away from this ghostly Greek messenger,
this Seer of truths,
Cassandra's brother, who should be believed.

Tulips

Tulips are impartial.

They open, sun-warmed,
caressed by breezes and eyes.
Colors a surety,
their silk- petal heartiness
a solid comfort to the touch.

Yes, they are impartial,
blooming in Europe
despite history and hatred,
haughty art, pretentious architecture,
arrogant politics.

They bloom in Illinois, too,
in humble yards with junk cars and broken swing sets,
along streets where nameless dogs roam for food;
and on the plains of Canada, approaching Quebec,
there are tulips, blooming for tourists and separatists.

Native Grecian flower, it blooms at the feet
of its dispirited citizens
grappling with austerity and hardship,
while the world holds its breath.
Taking to the streets, they shout their truths to police,
wield their anger at the air
while the tulips remain impartial,
though they are speaking.

Cold Stone

Cold stone seems to satisfy.

Press your hand against the wall.
Find the name.
Run your finger through the letters,
rub paper with pencil,
take it home.

His legacy is here
but he is nowhere,
and a heart is not enough to hold it.
You need cold stone,
a monument,
to show the world about existence.

Cold stone seems to satisfy.

Pillars, obelisks, statues spread out and set apart,
claim space, demand honor,
filling up the world where nature alone once spoke its piece.
Cold stone taking place of hands,
souls, smiles,
trees, flowers, grass.

This world needs cold stone.

Stand and Sing

The country mourns—perpetual now.
Flags wave in a half-heart-beat,
resolve unmasked at half- mast.

It is the dead of March
and winter's hand still holds the ground.
I hold ground, too, feet firmly planted in a difficult life.
Not budging, I stand against the world's oppression;
sign every lefty e-petition in the inbox,
donate my five, my ten to all who promise to help gain
back our lost freedoms,
heal the wounded,
comfort the hungry, the abused, the very confused.

It is a gape-mouthed world of need,
accepting each scrap tossed its way,
sucking up morsels and detritus, making no distinction.
Meanwhile profits from bake sales and raffles,
box-tops and labels collected by committed mothers,
act as hopeful expectation against a full budget of war.

But that loose change can't approach the One Percent's
hoard of half the country's wealth.
Won't add up to a semester's worth of tuition,
even at a community college.
Cards stacked, we dare not move too quickly, or all collapses.
Frozen, we feel ourselves cowards,
the word not sitting well in our American ears.

We must stand and sing.
Sing out loud, as Pete sang.
Bell for bell, tone for tone,
sound against the night,
against the day,
heads back, jaws wide,
chests filled with air.
We must sing our message of defiance.

Divine we rise, divine we sing.
Shoulder to shoulder
marching with truth, hands held out
anticipating justice,
blind, but ready to see—
ready to stare down the puffy, choleric eyes of those
working to snatch our freedoms,
wanting to grab them away, permission-less, with tiny hands,
devising ways to add our liberty to their collection
of worldly treasures.

How much would be enough?
How much land?
How much oil?
How much money?
How much power?

We must not wait for those answers.
We must stand together, and sing;
beat back their insatiable appetite.

"The problem we are confronting now is not one of right vs. left, republican vs. democrat…
the challenge we are confronting now is a challenge of pending tyranny." Robert Reich

**This poem was dedicated to folk singer and activist Pete Seeger on the 100th anniversary year of his birth.

Asking the Question

Asking the question is where valor lies.
It takes as much courage as killing an enemy,
while holding on to calm.

Surely the answer made him wince at first,
but when he knelt as the anthem played,
the many innocent dead stood by his side,
grateful for Kaepernick's silent protest.

My Friendly Neighborhood Nazi

First, it was a triangle of cloth,
pulled down over just one pane of garage door glass,
and that was surprising enough
but sometime last summer
the thing unfurled
and with it its misbegotten past
as the flag of Dixie was revealed in full.

This neighbor's house is pleasant,
a colorful brick, carefully decorated in each season--
once a one-room school house,
the pedigreed townies say,
blue bloods who claim their 300-year residencies.

On my afternoon walks he and his wife are often in the yard,
puttering, improving,
tending to their nasty little spaniel
who still barks at me
though you would think after all these years
he would recognize my old maroon coat,
my smell.
They never look up to smile hello and
I had learned to respect that,
the New England privacy thing,
though I,
daughter of the Midwest
still glance over, imagining one day I will get a simple nod.

Now I look at the flag,
haven't yet figured out my plan of action,
whether to go and finally have that first,
neighborly conversation,
try to sound them out,
listen for a space to leave a rational remark--
or just throw an egg at the window.

I would like to know what his beef is,

what his plan is, and think, perhaps,
I should share the recently confirmed news
given to me by DNA results,
that there's a bit of West Africa,
running through my Irish, British veins,
and I am
only a few feet away,
breathing his air.

Thoreau's Window

Henry David knew
beauty could be found
through a dirty window in a prison cell.
He lay all that long July night,
the window open
inside the grate of the whitewashed room
listening,
and he sensed his place as never before,
heard the voices of his neighbors and the villagers at the inn,
felt the heartbeat of his town,
put his hands on the thick stone walls
and anticipated the morning.

We must tame our pain first
to get back to our core
when life boomerangs us out
to unintended places
and once we do
 it is possible
to see beauty through a dirty window
and greet another morning.

Breaking the Firmament

I am not the one who wants to send more junk
into outer space,
a fake moon that would be brighter than the original,
or set up more 5-G towers to microwave messages
and who knows what else
to ourselves,
or play music on the H-A-A-R-P,
sending vibrations around the country,
messing with nature.
I am not the one dropping chemicals from planes
dripping with the prestige of Harvard Scientists,
nor an engineer from CERN who wants
to collide those atoms and mash and smash
those protons into other protons, trying to outdo Shiva.

I do not want to break the Firmament.
I only long to lie under it on a warm summer night,
 proximal to a bottle of good wine
as you, my finally found love,
 tangle your leg with mine.

All the Useless Things

Tire treads and snow boots leave
art deco patterns in the mud and moosh.
Lip balm hides in containers resembling fruit,
crayons smell like food,
yet we cannot feed everyone,
though we know how to grow,
how to store.

Singing fish and dancing Santa dolls fill
department store shelves,
cheap entertainment for the price of the plastic and batteries.

Trinkets cram the aisles,
a thousand things to amuse and beautify;
florescent, funny key chains,
glittery nail polish,
glo-sticks,
over-sized mugs,
under-sized shirts and yes,
I bought them, gave them to friends,
and laughed,
though I knew the dye went into the water,
the polyoxymethylene and the acetone and the phenol
degrade slowly,
and the workers in China have it bad.

Worse than I did that summer at the toy factory,
when the boss told me I couldn't
lean against a barrel to relieve my back,
while his girlfriend sat in a chair,
both of us tying knots into red and white striped ropes,
tossing them into barrels--
(never knew what the ropes were for).
I was educated that summer of '74,
standing all day on the cement floor
for my $3.15 hourly wage and so yes,
I know something about the global economy
and useless things.

Arms around Mother Nature

We are trying to comfort her,
this mother of ours whose cries are now audible to all;
even the most callous of souls can hear,
can see.

Scout troops pick up trash each spring and enterprising lads
make bracelets out of the plastic
they pluck from the ocean,
the profits creating equipment and jobs
to take away the thousands of pounds
of our modern conveniences
thoughtlessly tossed into her blue-green waters.
The well intentioned push to go straw-less,
recycle everything,
consolidate trips in the car,
walk more
need less.

She is burning.
She is flooding.
She is quaking.
She is choking on our dross.

We must tell her we care.
We must lie on her soft grass, hands out and say,
"We love you."
"We are sorry."
"Please forgive us."

Bus Ride

Incongruity.
The meaning is known,
but seeing so much around me
strains my eyes, my brain,
fogs my understanding.

From the window I see people hustle, run for busses,
sell their cakes, clay pots and drinks on the streets,
while others wither in doorways,
pressed against buildings,
hands held out, hoping for a coin, some food.
All equal in God's philosophy,
but ranked by the world.

Billboards shout their message that
new housing is coming
and you can buy or rent there soon,
or get an existing place now
in a huge structure of stone and glass,
while the rest of the ride brings me
to rubble-filled vacant lots
where proud and useful buildings once stood,
where people lived, and dreamed,
now just piles of debris, fodder for the landfill.

This is not a cycle.
This is not a progression.

This is the beat of life and destruction
that goes on all at once
together,
both together,
the freshly built and the condemned,
the hope of fulfillment,
the emptiness of despair,
the living and the dead.

Down in Dublin

It glistened green as promised--
mesmerizing jewel of legend, pain and perseverance.

Upside down I kissed the stone,
saw moss on the grey castle walls
and a row of golden helmets enshrined in a church;
tribute to war that takes all from those
leaning on the promise of heaven.

An old man played accordion for coins
atop the Ring of Kerry,
famine villages revealed their ghosts,
while down in Dublin we danced with locals
outside the Foggy Dew,
debated where to dine,
listened while Angela Murphy gave directions.

One thousand homeless sleep in Dublin,
sliver of the world's billion displaced and dreaming
under a common sky,
while fortunate emigrants
warm in beds with raw memories of Ireland.

Solitary, like the monks rising up
700 feet into the sky in the crags of Skellig Michael,
they wait on the day,
mourn the vanished,
try to feel the pluck of Dagda's harp.

Words of the Masters

Upheaval/fright/anger/confusion,

yet,

infinity, radiance, equanimity, jubilation.

* * *

Uncertainty/ loneliness/ sorrow/ grief,

yet,

laughter, reunions, rising, serenity.

* * *

Disease/ hunger/ endless war/ endless weapons/

endless war,

yet

friendship, odysseys, touching, transformation,

goodness,

kindness,

virtue,

wisdom,

unity,

love.

Christos

Wrap them, Christos.
Wrap them again,
buildings in Bern, Spoleto and Berlin.

Cover them in white, hide the rough stone,
the gargoyles, eagle's claws,
birds with beaks in an open scream.

Fabric's magician, cloak aggression and pride--
sail it into the past.
Startle into memory the beauty of a blank field,
 sun pouring through clouds,
sky revealed by 20 stories gone.

Force wonder at the reams and folds bound by soft cords,
gently moving against granite sides.
Make us marvel at your care to do this task---
revealing the story by what's obscured.

Wrap the stone buildings and calm the granite,
the limestone,
the pretentiousness of the past.
Help us to float in sheets of soft cloth to heaven.

Hungry

Everything is hungry.
Everything is tired.
Everything's been tried, washed and wiped dry.

Everyone is shifting, waiting,
afraid to speak their true mind.

These days we make sense of the impossible
and struggle to understand ourselves.
We sift through a steady stream of potions, lotions,
 stick-ons, cling-ons, pull-ons,
push-ups, zip-lids, flip-tops, fill-ins,
stand-ins,
phonies.

Have another drink, Holden, and I will
wait for you.

Stars

Hydrogen and helium blast and gas in a chain of endless nuclear explosions,
our sun's warmth welcome exchange for the danger.
Scientists think Solis is 8.3 light minutes away,
(the distance between unrequited lovers),
so this is truly far.

Nine thousand stars are visible with natural eyes;
Proxima and Alpha Centauri,
Barnard's Star, Wolf 359,
 Lalande 21185 and Sirius among the top ten.
Their shimmery past journeys to us,
and we marvel at this mysterious, lost message.
Others churn in the firmament, out of view
while NASA makes plans to reach them--
discover the rest of their secrets.

 But I am an ancient Greek on a Thessalonian shore
when searching the night sky,
watch Orion stand against the charge of Taurus;
regard Ursa Major and her cub,
ponder why vain, neglectful Casseopia
would sacrifice her daughter.

Scientists calculate the possibilities
of reaching Alpha Centauri,
believe it could happen in 44 years
once we learn to travel
at even 10 percent of the speed of light,
and a Russian billionaire has imagined
a spacecraft the size of a computer chip
that could make the 40 trillion kilometer climb;
he envisions anti-matter meeting matter,
pictures that chip-ship riding the thermonuclear blast.
Experts talk of high-powered lasers,
catalyzed fusion,
the Bussard ramjet,
a way to compress hydrogen for the necessary thrust,

harvesting fuel as they go.

But I am a native on the continent,
clad in deer skin,
tired from hunting and sated with the feast.
Lying on the summer ground I hear the owl's deep call,
stare up at all those stars that tell me what science never will.

Planets

Maybe if we could see them,
giant pendants filling naked eyes,
we would finally accept the force
more powerful than ego, hunger,
 violence, desire, death.
A force equal to dreams that binds and heals,
benevolent and watchful.

More are discovered all the time:
Orcus, Haumea, Makemake.
One a golden consciousness, one an oath of the soul.
Quaoar, the sacredness of life, and nature's way, Varuna,
appear in the telescope's lens.
Exiled, feminine Sedna floats in icy Oort Cloud dust,
existing on the perimeter of space
just as her Earth bound sisters
drift on the edges of men's lives and their politics.
Ixion and Eris, one a titan, one a disrupter,
create dwarfs of former full-bodied planets---
intentions unclear.

And there is j147b whose rings swirl out like a dervish skirt,
200 times Saturn and far beyond its realm.
Daily sight of these orbs might make us pause each day
before the next petty slight, public lie,
bomb drop from a drone.
If it were closer,
j147b would seem a city in the sky, many times the moon,
a suspended altar ready for our sacrifice.
An indisputable reminder,
more than the accepted sun and its underestimated partner,
that there is more than we.

Roseland Park—Fall Morning

Wisps of fog twist away,
revealing a blae plate of a lake.
Troops of happy, hungry squirrels gather,
while a fish pushes one clean ripple to the surface;
a quiet sound of still water, disturbed.

A stolen moment,
this view of lifting mist off Roseland Lake;
skipping work, skipping school,
healing self and soul.

Town looks better this way—
 obscured, dissolved, softened,
sun beaming through shredded cotton clouds.
The decayed boat launch is visible
from my bench—quiet reminder
of heydays, before milfoil
choked out the swimming.

More is visible now and
they are trees-- not mountains;
but if I squint I can still pretend.

A plane leaves its trail, the end becoming
an Arabic scroll of goodbye as it heads north.
Only hunger will drive me from this place,
as I possess all time on this stolen day.

Legacy

We have the Pompei dog,
DaVinci's paintings,
Shakespeare's gloves,
 the 32 plays, the 154 sonnets.

We have world-wide ruins where people
baked bread, told tales, fought with and loved
 their children and friends.
 Feudal swords hang on walls in Japan,
the hands that wielded them
rested into dust.
Eyes in ancient mid-eastern mosaics
still look out on scenes where people once passed;
thousands of vanished people.

And we have grandma's cut glass sugar bowl,
 her leather bound Rubaiyat,
her lace scarf legacy,
her lessons of love.

Roman Ruin

Like an ancient ruin it stands--
memento of the Industrial age,
now a perch for brave birds.
Smooth, this yellow brick forgotten tower
once belched smoke,
as girls on the factory floor
sweated over their bobbins, shuttles and molds,
turning out thread, cloth, trays of buttons.

Counterpoint to the rot of this old mill town,
the pillar is Vitruvian, majestic,
a dark crown of crows lounging on its rim,
satisfied with their view.
Twenty-five years of life lived here,
but I only really saw it yesterday.

Rome was a surprise, too.
Locals ran their errands, unimpressed by antiquity,
while we stood still,
gaping at the remains of the past,
columns and arches enough to imagine that other world,
2,000 years away.
Traffic flowed, people walked their dogs,
past and present fused together,
and we marveled at time's appetite,
vanished possessions,
families turned to ancestors.

The Eye

Giant wheel moves 'round,
then slows letting the others on.

All is a wheel turning in measured moments,
so continual you don't notice right away
how it takes you from the familiar to the unimagined.

Point of view is your only compass.
What is good?
What is bad?

Standing in The Eye we viewed
London's buildings and bridges,
but not through walls or into the minds and plots of others.

It moved round, weather changed, clouding heaven's gaze.
Twenty minutes brought biting wind, cold rain, pelting hail.
Brief excitement, and I was happy
I brought those gloves.

Spanish Town

I want to stand in a dusty Spanish town at one o'clock,
the hottest of the day,
when lunch makes bellies heavy,
thoughts fog and streets clear as people head for siestas,
the hum of unseen bugs playing ancient music.

Sit in a round-backed, wooden chair at a street café.
Sip impossibly bitter coffee from a tiny, porcelain cup,
decaled with a pattern I would never choose.
Watch locals bring their children and packages home,
glimpse lovers walking out of warm stone buildings
on their way to supper,
as shadows climb across the streets.

Could find renewal in an unknown place,
letting mysteries flow over me,
language and music,
dust of other pasts settling on my shoulders,
breathe in the mist from a different sea.
Might free myself from attached expectations;
ready myself for a Revolution.

Montecatini

We tumbled from the tour bus,
checked in at the front desk,
agreed to meet for dinner at 6.

"The hotel is old," the clerk said,
"and was very well-known in its day."
"Look, here's the plaque," he pointed,
proving that important men once stayed here;
wealthy, learned men.

The 1880 elevators were too narrow,
too few, and slow,
so we carried our suitcases
up three flights of stairs,
realizing the worth of 50 pounds.
Our room was spacious, though oddly construed,
wallpaper textured like grey sand.

You claimed your side of the bed,
threw a few things in drawers,
went out to shop with Anna.
But I was not 30, I was 52,
so I kicked off my shoes,
washed my face and readied for
an hour of freedom.

The room had a small window,
shuttered in green wood.
I pushed the shutters open,
looked down at the ancient Italian street,
saw the cake shop and the park.
You and Anna walked fast, heading to the square.

Later, sitting on the bed with my journal,
trying to capture something of the day,
the 5 o'clock church bells rang
just as they had in medieval times--
and I was alone in Montecatini.

Grecian Dream

All the sensible people are home it seems,
for I am walking alone on Kennedy Drive.

February's blast is returned and
I want to see the water; not the blue Aegean,
just the brackish, dark river
that flows through this little town.

It is one o'clock on Sunday, and I seek
the sting of that zero degrees;
prove I am alive.

I am of course, alive, though not always happily so.
Like me, all is dried and broken,
brown, crunched.
It will take a long, patient spring to heal this ground.

Voices on the radio
keep me apprised of daily troubles and horror.
People burn in the streets; flags and anger.
Even my dream of Greece is a shill,
for though the sea might still be cerulean,
the air is fraught with debt and tension.
Would peace even be at the ouzo bottle's bottom,
eyes closed under an Athenian sun?

Ahead I see the falls, a torrent of endless, cascading water.
Its power goes inside me, and for a while I sense hope.

Then, the cold makes me a believer again
in heaven and hearth.
I must go home.

Iron and Dust

She is doing what I still do, ironing clothes,
though more than a century parts the task.
"Woman irons on Dugg Hill Road," the caption read.

I drive that road, the pinnacle of town
presenting a panorama of the quiet valley
in the "Quiet Corner."
Sunsets wait there when I tire of my spot in the woods
where treetops grab the colors, drag them too early to earth.

She holds a flat iron, hot from the woodstove.
Hair piled in the mandatory 1908 bun,
shirtwaist on her frame, sleeves rolled up;
a Gibson girl of beauty and strength.
The window is open. It is summer.
Flowers are on the table and a curly-haired child
sits on the floor in rumpled, cotton clothes.

She irons with determined expectation.
It is her duty.
This is something that matters.
This chore is a correction.
We are linked in this,
though my prideful ironing has diminished over years,
lessons from jersey knit and perma-press
broadening my philosophy.
She does not have the luxury.
She must press and press,
leaning over the steam for long minutes,
making right what the washtub and the clothes line
made wrong.
Hold up the front to fit in,
place a firm foot forward in a shifting world.

Sometimes I look for her house as I drive by,
wonder which one it was.
I want to whisper over her lawn, over the years,
something of sisterhood,
something about smooth, clean cloth.

The Great Divide

Sometimes it was that third pair of "nice" jeans,
or two good and fashionable coats
separating one girl from another.
It was professional fathers, homes in the suburbs,
their moms shopping slow, reading books in the afternoon,
while ours charged out the door
to be on the factory floor by 7 a.m.
It was having 50 bucks to blow instead of ten,
shoplifting because they were bored and reckless,
not simply imagining what the bracelet would look like
on their wrist.

The future was theirs, no matter what.
Firmly placed connections
making a wrong move impossible;
a birthright of confidence,
while the rest of us, motivated by hunger and a smart fear
knew panning for gold would be rough and dangerous work.

But we could remember when a flower was a world,
those worlds made a chain,
the chain became a necklace, and the necklace was a gift.
A powdered donut filled your fist,
an ice cream was always too big,
melting fast,
dripping down the backs of your hands,
between your knees as you sat on the curb,
sometimes collapsing altogether,
wasted sweetness on the hot sidewalk.
Butterflies, a wonder,
lightning bugs friends you could borrow for the night
and then free.

Song and silence filled the same need,
beauty was love and love was beautiful.
Happiness no more than a bike ride
or a nudge from a friend,
sadness only twilight, the day's end.

Hunger in the belly, not yet in the mind,
we repaired our weariness with sleep,
satisfied with simplicity and nature,
unaware yet of the divide.

Crepe Paper Proms

Haven't really understood how cars work,
cows sleep, or what yogis eat.

Haven't always known what to say in hospitals,
at wakes or when people feign interest.

Haven't often been sure what to wear,
which side to part my hair,
or the steps to that dance they do at weddings.

Wasn't schooled in social graces,
simply told to just say "Thank you,"
and to keep my slip from showing.

There were no dinner parties,
no elegant events in my girlhood,
just crepe paper proms in the gym
and church basement receptions
with cake and sugared punch.

Now, fifty years have passed and
as I seek to put order to the profound and the pointless,
I make sure to laugh out loud as often as possible.

Tough Girls

We were a little afraid of those girls--
tough girls in our town--
the life they came from.

Lank hair, wiry bodies with taut faces,
expressions hardened by scant meals,
their eyes plunged through ours
as they sized us up,
black liquid eyeliner worn like war paint--
a warning:

"Don't fuck with me," it said.

By 14 they knew things we did not:

Cornflakes could be eaten for supper.
Clothes could be washed out in the sink with
a bar of soap.
Swiping a lipstick or some gum
from the drug store
was pretty easy; that you could cry
and hold your breath
at the same time.

They could get the coat and boots off their dad,
and put him to bed.
They learned where their mom kept her money stash
and cigarettes,
 when not to let the neighbor boys in the house, and how to
turn an uncle's old jacket into a fashion statement.

As high school rolled on we noticed
them dropping away, petals from a wilting flower.
No longer in class—no longer in the bleachers at games—
no longer haunting Main Street with their Cimmerian eyes.

Some Nights

There were ways to survive it--
small town life.
It required shoe leather,
empty basements with record players and a couch,
Boones Farm, a six pack, some smokes;
John, Linda, Bob and James to sing us what was true.

It required thermoses full of sloe gin fizz,
shrimp baskets from Robert's Drive Inn,
Monty Python at 10 p.m. on Sunday,
the carnival every June, part-time jobs.

We had been to church; were baptized and confirmed.
Did good up to a point.
Then we awakened to our dad's dead end jobs and our
mother's endless desires for a new car, a new winter coat
and a finished basement; their longings for paved driveways
they could ride on into society
weighed down our hearts.

We weren't sure what that meant for us,
but the time clock in the factory taught us our worth,
and some nights we climbed up on the hood of the car,
watched the sun go down into the cornfield
and planned our escape.

Down Home

Interstate 55 cuts an artery southwest
through dark Illinois fields,
'cross train tracks, 'longside silos big as dinosaurs,
grain enough to feed a county,
empty as drums in hard times.
From Springfield Dad takes 72 then on to 67
past Winchester, Manchester.
We get excited. Know that soon we'll be out of the car,
can untangle from each other, stand up and pull our damp
clothes from our sweaty limbs.
It is summer, 1967, and we are heading "down home."
Dad's car has no air conditioner and our ears
hurt from the sound of the hard road
through the open windows,
my ponytail blown into a tangle,
both tired from trying to sit in the back seat
without touching.

Three hundred miles is a long way,
but we make the trek every summer to see
Grandma and Grandpa,
cousins we don't really know,
visit places from our parents' past.
These roads were taken north as a sacrifice,
a drive toward a better life,
but one that left much unsettled in the country dust.
Now we ride on, see the beguiling, smiling Sunbeam girl
biting into that fresh slice of bread,
her billboard face flanked by telephone poles,
their thin arms outstretched in a summer welcome.

Roodhouse

I went back to Roodhouse,
scratch of roads in the Illinois soil,
with my husband and my kids.
It was a bombed-out Beirut of a place,
backstreets full of trash,
smashed glass and porch socials.
Teen moms in extra-large T-shirts
holding dull and dirty babies on their laps
never smiled as they sat
waiting for something to happen.

It was summer, but there was no green,
just the colored metal cars
lining the streets.
Two for each house, but one don't work.
No breeze,
yet the sound of television
did waft through the neighborhood,
and the submerged sun
did give off some heat.

We drove slow through the square
eyes blighted by chipped red brick and
duct taped panes of glass
in shops where I had set foot
as a girl. Even then, things were
worn down,
but not out.

There are ghosts in Roodhouse, I could see them.
They sat in Mike Todd's diner where teens
met on a Friday night,
and at the feed store
where men gathered to read the paper and chew.
Ladies in prim knee-length dresses
and sharp little hats traveled from
the pharmacy to the butcher, to the beauty parlor
and the library,

and in the park benches painted thick with enamel green
waited for tired 1940 feet to rest.

And Grandma and Mrs. Kemp were only there in memory,
no longer feeding children and chickens.

Cornfields

They were the best jobs in the county,
paying more than minimum wage;
made us a little smug.

Hard work in those fields,
days of sunburn and sweat,
but we were energetic,
kids with aspirations and
weekend plans.
Endurance was easy.
Stomping around in the citrine passageways,
we watched the corn grow through the glacial gift
beneath our feet,
deep and soft, like chocolate cake.
We labored under heaven's blazing gaze,
and the observant eyes of the boss
adding our hourly wage in our heads.

Rainy days we'd stay in the shed,
put things in order while top 40 hits
repeated every hour on the radio. When skies cleared,
Elmer's relic of a tractor brought us back to the fields,
our legs swinging off the flatbed in a silent rhythm.

The leaves would kiss my arm as I walked the rows,
a gentle acknowledgement,
each aisle distinct and known by season's end.
I loved the fields, the wind, my friends,
the water fights, the quiet rides home in the truck,
all of us bonded with pollen and fatigue.

Some tended the good corn while others offered death,
plagued the plants with bores and bugs,
poked them with fungus-coated sticks to see
who would stand,
who could survive the disease,
the heat, the rain.

Questioning nothing, we modified everything.
We finished college, paid back the loans, learned to survive.
We are still outlasting the storm.

Saturday Night at the Shamrock
(Ode to an old favorite bar)

Winter west of Chicago hosts black prairie nights,
relentless wind,
snow frozen to the edges of sidewalks,
edges of smiles.
Down on Lincoln Highway
half-a-dozen taverns fill in space between the shops.
Our favorite is The Shamrock where we warm bones,
play pool, drink cheap beer and dance.

Low, gold light pours through diamond panes
in the dark wood door
that pushes into a great room, dim and comforting,
forgiving flaws and foolishness.
The black-stained oak, varnished to gloss
lets 40 years of prints and pints be wiped away.
Tudor décor surrounds us
with the flavor of Medieval Europe,
though we sit in Illinois.

There are regulars.
We are regulars, too; know not to sit at the corner of the bar.
That seat belongs to "The Chief,"
a russet-haired, Vietnam Vet,
keeper of good vinyl at the Record Revolution.
He sits alone, speaks only to the bartender,
watches our antics with a void expression.

Saturday is special when Batista's band plays,
a shot of electric funk for the craving crowd.

We always sit on the main floor, never in the balcony.
We are there early enough to get a table, share our chairs
and dance, dance, dance until the band can play no more.
The beat is mild, reggae infused, livable.
Moving out into the smoky air, we sway in time,
become an amorphous, pulsating amoeba--
twist, get low, and shake it back up to

float again among the gathering.
Sweaty, satisfied, we are not sad when the lights come up
and it's last call.
We have another drink though there is no need;
won't feel the cold going home.
It is Saturday night at The Shamrock, and now
we'll make it till Tuesday,
when we will come again to drink the 30 cent beers.

Asleep in the Field

The day was cloudy,
so we nixed the beach walk
and went to the local sanctuary,
a few plots of farmland and a forest-rimmed ravine
creating a haven for butterflies,
birds and what's left of the bees,
protected now by well-written grants.

You pulled your hood up over your hat
and I was glad to have remembered my scarf
because it was a damp cold
seeping into our clothes and bones.

Colors are muted now.
October ran by so fast
I feel I missed it,
though photographic proof shows I was there.
Now the goldenrod is all champagne seeds,
some leaves are curled backwards
revealing their ivory underside
and all is hushed and crackling,
dried to a hundred shades of brown,
while there in the field,
surrounded by a carefully placed stonewall,
a family was sleeping in the ground they once tilled,
and the headstones whispered what was erased
by time and the elements,
as we quietly walked away.

Spoken Word
(for Wendy)

Two young, single girls on a Saturday.
Your old station wagon named George
and your black lab named Blue,
we were feeling good and free
as we set out toward
Issaquah
to get out of the city
out of our 9 to 5
and into an adventure.

It is years ago now.
I remember I didn't have
hiking boots,
just my old college snow boots,
scuffed faux leather with red laces and spongy souls,
and it was fall,
cloudy and dramatic like it is in the Northwest.

Hiking deep into the trees,
off of an old logging road
we came out on a ledge,
sat to eat our sandwiches and
my 35 millimeter rolled down to the bottom of the ravine,
but smart Blue went down and got the thing.

After lunch we hiked a little higher
and there was a moment when we both stopped short
because we heard it at the same time.
Not a sound,
but a thought coming from
a giant fir tree,
and you grinned at me
because trees always talked to you,
but it was my first time.

Portrait

A dance mom, a teacher, a sometimes sullen wife,
loving invested mother,
cool sister,
absent daughter.

A Christian, rethinking her position.
A student of philosophy and jive- pop psychology.
A rainmaker, a wound dresser,
a cake baker, mender of socks and emotions.
Blender of truth and hope.

A friend of Isadora.
A hostess.
A party-girl.
Gloria's apprentice.
A wild and reckless heart
buried under wall-to-wall carpet
in a finished basement.
A woman with survival strategies,
duct tape and a sewing kit.

A gash, a sore, a scar.

Hell, dozens of scars.

A waitress
waiting on tables of regret and
banquets of redress.

A morning of hope after a night of despair.
A warm hand, a kiss,
a final question as you go out the door.
A steady hand to hold the pan
as you take your portion.
A mirthful apple, sweet and wise,
waiting on the highest branch.

What Summer Was

Walking out the pain and boredom of a day's work
I see the lavender underbelly of the clouds.
Cushions of airy, caramel pine needles meet my feet while
my eyes take in dried leaves curling into mauve cocoons,
tiny containers of summer's memory.

Was it happy?
More logistics than fun, really.
We are people who share cars, leftovers, sweaters,
look for a corner of the room to sit undisturbed,
negotiate tasks for free time:
the picking up, the dropping off.
We tend to scrape, paint and repair
our vacations away.

As a girl I enviously read stories
where people spent a month by the sea,
or a summer in the mountains by a cool, quiet lake.
Now I think it would be dangerous to go that long—
could I return to my stifling routine after such freedom?

Last summer we rented a vacation house for a week;
it looked down upon an inlet and on the back porch
we sat with coffee in the morning,
watched boats cruise along,
and evenings, we poured glasses of wine,
waited for the moon to send its light into the water,
saw it dance on the waves, heard the night birds.
A week without scraping and painting.
A week without negotiations.

Now that time is done and I see
the mash up of fall colors—
amber, topaz, garnet, brick, rioting on the green.
One more walk toward the darkest day of the year.
One more tour of the neighborhood before the slight chill
turns to a threat on survival,
and thoughts of summer become a beacon again.

Pulling Rank

Out of the sun but into the light,
sunblock in my left eye
I was so clever to wait for everyone to go
so as to be left
alone.

All one.

To write....writing often preferable
to some stilted conversation
where I bear the burden of rank as mother
to make everyone feel good about themselves,
feel that things will
be all right.

Hell, I'm pretending half the time myself,
but have gotten really good at it.

Sometimes if you pretend enough
the tale becomes true.
Happens all the time to
criminals
and salesmen.

Light Bearers

The golden boughs of the bushes on Robbins Road
cast a gentle, sun-filled glow.
Limbs of light, worthy for a crown of thorns;
hat for a savior's head.

Holy and humble,
these branches lack a bloom in this steady, cold spring,
no leap made yet into the warmer clime,
only an unreliable promise of toasty goodness to
heal the frozen masses,
the stuck and muddy grass waiting, too.

It was a hard winter, with hard truths.
No, no one died—just moved away,
taking their smells and peccadillos with them,
leaving longing and relief in equal parts.

To love that much is metamorphic rock,
rugged, multi-colored toughness,
not smooth, cool granite where a daily dust of troubles
can be wiped away,
but craggy, catching all the errors of love,
never letting them go—never really forgiving anything,
remembrance deep in each pitted place,
where "sorry" echoes back, a missed intention.

Older

Wisdom, they say, comes with time.

Well, there has been time enough.

Time enough to push through romantic dross,
sift fiction from wheat,
take the heavy grain-- make bread,
if not love.

Time enough to push into the future,
exploding into each full and frantic day of jobs and
bills and errands and cats and children
and myriad disconnected people,
hoping still
things would get better.

There has been enough time to learn
appreciation for little things;
titanium-winged dragon flies,
tree trunk shadows,
soft wind, and the complete stillness of an algae-laden pond.

Time to marvel at the wrinkles on a stranger's face,
the note left by a daughter; the glance you once gave me.
Time to love the sharp taste of lemon,
the smell inside an old book,
the memory of how the baby's cheek once felt
against my thumb.

Dark Color

It is blue.
Not tropical fish blue,
but that inky, ball point pen blue,
the kind you get on your hands
when the damn thing explodes.

Sticky, wet, ineffaceable blue.

By the standards of this world
I have everything.
 I have most things, and the promise of getting
more things, more experiences,
and reasonable health,
so letting this Midnight-Prussian-Oxford blue wash over me
and through me
and allowing myself to swim in it
all day
 seems selfish and I feel loathsome
but tonight there is no way out of the dark color of regret.

Sometimes its not enough to say "things could be worse,"
when you long for how it all could have been better.

The Wheel has Turned

It moved other day with me,
standing in my kitchen
of all places.

Not an extraordinary spot to feel
that wheel shift the story,
the tumult and turn
of life against life,
but I felt it all the same.

Pivotal moments flashed past.
Decisive moments when
outside forces knocked
but the impact was yet unrealized,
unimagined, unknown.

Back when life was moving fast and I,
doing my part to keep up,
didn't always know that
things had been forever changed
by that turn of the wheel;
it was the last look,
the last fight, the final move,
the final phone call.

And so the odd remark or
the sideways glance
was noticed,
but not noted.

Not noted for what it was;
the turn of the wheel.

Not so now. Now I feel that wheel of karma
grind and hum under my feet and
I know exactly
where the invisible but solid

line has been drawn, marking where nothing will ever be the same, and where no one will remain in the place they used to be comfortably found.

Superposition

I stand in superposition,
alive and dead at the same time.

Like that cat.

The one in the experiment that
huffed the potion and was
alive and dead
until someone came,
took the lid off the box, looked inside.

"Really dead," someone said.

You have all gone and I am simply waiting
for someone to come, open the door,
look inside, and make a declarative statement.

The Evidence

The evidence of 30 years pulls apart in my hands.
These are your baby pictures
falling out of the album now,
glue at the edges dried into a crumbly dust.

You have turned 30.

I feel it in my body now as small pains and stiffness creep in,
but my mind resists this truth and the weight of "thirty"
impresses me; seems unreal.
In one picture your small head lay cradled by just one of
your father's hands;
you look up, a solemn, sleepy expression
on your little melon face,
and I remember that blue sleeper though I don't remember
taking the photo.
What is remembered is all that lovely time I spent with you,
my first child, my son,
the one who helped me plant my feet
more firmly in this carnival of a world,
with my new identity.

Not Alice

It wasn't sudden,
and mourning did occur
when I wasn't feeling just simple relief
at being finished with all those
motherly duties,
yet,
I sometimes now stand in the house,
and sense a white rabbit has run through my life,
that I've been to a Mad Hatter's Tea,
drunk something strange
and come out through the Looking Glass.

Checked Out

"Send a picture."
He said it twice.
And then I got it—
this ex-o-mine wanted to
Ex-a-mine me
and see if
I was fat or what,
or if he
had
made a
mistake.

Facing Grain

Facing grain I hear
years of forest growth telling tales.
Elongated patterns of sliced wood between us,
you are now my closed door.
Too much to balance, the act and the history.
Too many people involved in our complication.
A long time coming, this.

A see-saw between us we stood on opposite ends,
slowly worked our way to the middle till
you pushed me off.
A child's game.
A child's decision.

Thirty years is three times ten.
Which window and where
will open?

Birds Fallen

5,000 birds have fallen,
tumbled from the sky,
yet you are why I cannot sleep.

Pyramids of snow in hand
your eyes bore through me
from the frozen page.

Archeology

The past still lets me dig there whenever I want.
There is muck to hoe.

Sometimes the excavation unearths the deal breaker.

Like that guy putting his tongue in my ear
as we hugged goodnight on the first date,
(after I paid for the meal),
or the slow realization how materialistic
my best friend had become,
or the night you tore the collar off my shirt,
and I realized the next time
would probably be a punch.

Thirty days later I moved out,
but your litany of excuses followed me
much longer while your life eroded.
Finally, I learned protecting myself
meant not listening to you anymore,
not pretending I could actually help,
though I did take that old cat off your hands for a while.

We Have Become Something

We have become something unintended,
starting as we did on a raft of hope
sailing into the void of the world,
unaware of our fate, but grabbing as much Destiny
as our small hands could hold.

We have become something.

We sheared off excess views,
dreams, possessions,
obsessions,
and leaner, we pitched forward into
days and nights
determined to survive.
We have become men, women, leaders,
followers,
passive,
aggressive,
determined,
weary.
Found the journey daunting and full of
subtle dangers; eye rolls, head nods, dropped voices,
rumors,
lies,
the savage danger of jealousy.

Who are you to attempt happiness?
Cut you with looks and silence,
with avoidance, such good Christians, all.

We have become something not intended.
Surviving the slights, the slaps, pinches,
cheap shots.
We have withstood it all to proclaim our truth:
we are worthy of life,
we are keeping our joy.
We are keeping our joy.

The Middle

So....this is the middle.
The middle of life, the middle of the day,
middle of the year....(well, ok, it's August.)

And, I am disgruntled.

Others might say, "witch-like."

And I have questions,
like:

"Is this the middle of a plan,
or is this the beginning of another tough lesson?"
"Is this the middle of a flower, a walk, or a sandwich?"
"Is this the middle of a book, a chapter or a verse?"
"Is this "middle" something to be celebrated
or a thing to be walked around?"

Yes, I have questions.

"Is this the middle of a field with dreams around it,
or a dream in the center of a field?
If it is a field, are those dreams
still going to remain out of reach,
 or will my arms finally stretch enough,
 allow my fingertips to touch them,
inch them close enough to grab?"

"Is this middle a solid place to lay a foot,
 or is it squishy and muck-like?"

"Does this middle have a worthy direction,
or should it change course and go for something else?"

"Does this middle want to phone a friend,
 or just get a shout-out from the street?
And if it does win the money,
should it go for the double-or-nothing video challenge,

or just walk away with a sure thing?"

Was there ever a "sure thing?"

Paper Bag

The liveliest red,
(Revlon's best)
mushed near vivid orange,
nestled near tender pink,
a dash of passionate purple residing inside.

Outwardly, she is a brown, dry oak leaf.
Sturdy, dependable,
like a paper grocery bag,
soft from repeated folding,
though still good for use
despite the creases and a frayed edge.

Strong, like the dining table legs,
built to take some kicks,
able to hide the mar with a little stain,
some wax.

A pear is enfolding her former size 8,
size 10,
size 12 self,
squeezing away
the will to wear pantyhose.

Not much where it used to be.

Things have been placed in another room.

Her life has become like the 5-CD player;
enjoyable at first,
but now no one can bother
taking the discs out of the machine,
finding the cases,
alphabetizing them.

Yeah.
Done with pantyhose.
So done.

Process Processing

I am a process processing,
combination of waves and particles,
flesh and pheromones,
metabolism and respiration
though sometimes I feel quite clever,
make a bon mot,
snag a good sale,
hit a high note,
get an appreciative look.

But I am a walking cauldron of systems doing what they will,
day by day,
year by year,
with no regard for how I feel about any of it;
the flabby stomach,
the wrinkled neck,
the 4 p.m. exhaustion.

I am on their ride
these chemical arrangements
that leave me
frustrated with the realization
there will never be enough time
to live fully
to see it all and eat it all and be it all.
But I am doing what I can,
here inside my little personal Dutch Oven.

Gas Pump

Besides dealing with the big revival in 70's in clothing,
society's craving for mid- century modern furniture
and the endless sounds of classic rock
that dog me wherever I go,
my life now flashes before me whenever I put $20 dollars of
gas in my car.

Standing at the pump the years roll over,
slow enough to let me reflect as the numbers approach my
budgeted amount;
$19.70, $19.71, '72, '3, '4, and that summer before college,
(those stories for another time),
'75, 6, 7, 8, graduation and those first real jobs,
sleazy bosses, a beater car, great friends
and that first disastrous marriage.
Married and divorced by 24; at least I had the guts to leave.

Still holding the handle it's now the early 80's and I watch
my renewed commitment to staying single roll across the
small black screen,
until its 1984 and I meet you at work.
A nice guy. Kinda cute. You kept walking me home.
Finally, one night, I let you in.
Thirty years later we are still side by side.

 The pump speeds up to 2000 (twenty dollars) and shuts off,
but our lives didn't stop there.
We have made the most of those years
since you won me over
with a dinner of homemade stuffed peppers,
bird calls and wicked humor.
Still, I kind of wish gas would go to $3.00 a gallon
and give my brain a rest from the past.

Unexpected Friend

An obvious commonality,
something was strangely familiar in your manner,
your humor,
your pain.

It took me aback.

Me, who knows not to be fooled by shiny surfaces,
whose severe lessons burned away
pretense and some dreams,
my far-flung psyche gathered back slowly
through surrender, prayer, rediscovered self-love.

Not all had to travel that road.

Standing with you I sense acceptance.
No need to explain; everything understood, acknowledged.
A feeling of ease and grace after so much struggle,
my unexpected friend.

Cardinal Point

Velvet bird,
blood drop in aureolin leaves,
master of the yard for seconds at a time.

Only the bold sit at length,
all the small and bright ones are amaranthine,
enjoying life in swift microseconds
 lest it end.

Don't they get dizzy?
Where do they go
 when exhausted by this ceaselessness
they must stop and breathe?

That cardinal gets me thinking
each time I see it,
that he is telling me something
important,
making a prime point
that remains abstruse to me.

Yesterday's snow hugs the ground,
sticks to the roof tops and random outdoor furniture,
refuses to give up,
turn to vapor,
same as my ghosts
who climb into the car with me,
ride around town,
sit with me in coffee shops
and dog me home,
wait for their favorite TV show.

They won't be exorcised,
won't be soothed.
No new age wisdom, sweat lodges or shopping sprees
can jog them loose.
They cling fast like that slush in the shadows,
vibrating their relentless demands.

End of the World

Don't try to scare me that its the end of the World.
My world has already ended
multiple times,
and started up again,
old sights and sounds changed into
new ones, and familiar folks
disappeared and replaced by others,
souls I didn't know and wasn't even looking for.
Jobs have come and gone,
fun has come and gone and come again,
so you can't scare me with this hand wringing,
this bell clanging, this alarmed message that it will all end!
It has ended, over and over again,
and I have learned to hang on to what's meaningful
as I hurl through this carnival ride
taking it all in, eating my white cheddar cheese popcorn,
drinking my Miller, sometimes a Guinness,
sometimes a Blue Moon.

Lawn Chair

Life from a lawn chair can be lived in full.
Listen! Birds are speaking.
They don't mind if you try to crack the code.

Sun and cloud pass overhead.
Acknowledge them from your lowly, prone position,
or not,
for they are moving on, no matter what you do.

Rest. Rest.
Let the cats come circle the chair,
lie beside you.
Feel all the bits of rebirth poking through
the crunched detritus of winter,
green babies forcing life back into all; buds, shoots, stalks.
See parachute puffs of seeds drift toward tender spots to
land and grow.
They fly all around you in your chair, and you fly, too,
race to other times, other places, other springs,
when the humid warmth, the breeze,
the deep scent of fields filled your senses, and you lived
as Spring,
running free, shoes off, hair wild behind you,
living as sky, as earth, as wind.

The Apple

I

The apple in Eve's hand
felt cool and round.
She had no agenda
standing there,
enchanted by all she saw and
perceived around her.

The soft spring breeze lifted her hair,
breathed a welcome on the back of her neck
and wrapped around the garden,
around the tree.

The smooth, flame-colored apple
called her to take it—
encouraged her to make a claim
of delight and knowledge.
Spoke its promise to her—
a promise of wisdom and power.

She tugged slightly, and the fruit
 yielded its place on the branch
sliding into her hand.
She smiled, and thought
she had done a good thing.

II

The cell phone in her hand
felt cool and smooth.
Her only agenda standing there
was to connect—
to be with someone who understood.

She heard the radio and
the muffled voices of her family
coming from down the hall.

She pressed the keys, conscious of
a windy winter howl wrapping around the house.

Hitting the send button she felt encouraged
to make her claim
on this surprising relationship
that had grown quietly and unnoticed for many years;
beautiful now—ripe and mature,
promising knowledge, wisdom and power.

Holding the phone to her ear she smiled
as the voice of the other soothed her desire,
and she felt satisfied with what she had done.

Living Out Loud

Bright-bright
everything turned up loud,
color, texture--
a sense of coming out of one's seat,
one's skin,
one's secret past.

Looking up and out
through the windshield
the force of the light
and the shining, opalescent clouds
framed by trees rimmed with
ruby, emerald and gold
made me gasp,
"Ah, so beautiful!"

You agreed.

What else was there to say
or do
but keep driving down the road
into all that brilliant splendor?

Phone Call

Corey Monteith is dead,
but you're not dead
and I'm not dead.

Trayvon Martin is dead,
but you're not dead and I'm not
dead.

Fluxus is dead,
but I'm not dead and
you're
simply
unavailable.

Blue Coat

It will take you away soon,
that car I taught you to drive,
and that coat I helped you buy
will keep you warm on those
northern delta nights;
a blue, wool coat laying on the chair.

Sign of departure—that blue coat.

But here in the New World
automobiles will not drive me from my troubles,
and none of my coats will keep out winter's bite,
the songs on the radio incapable of preventing
my head from filling with thoughts of you,
while you spend your youth
without me,
in a foreign frenzy
like so much monopoly money.

Emily

Emily was right to tell me a thing so dreadful
could be endured.
But the double-day did not block my eyes with horror.
Rather, it opened them wide to view all the corners
where we have stood,
to see again all the chance and happy meetings
while snaps of conversations,
smiles exchanged and touches given
roll over all routine thought.

The tang and the sweet not always mixed in halves.

But your leaving did not block my eyes.

(This poem is derived from Emily Dickinson's "The First Day's Night Had Come.")

The Circus

Twirling, jumping, flying,
hanging by an arm, a leg,
spinning upside down,
smiling like they were simply combing their hair,
the acrobats displayed desired composure.
The juggler mastered six silver clubs,
dropped the seventh.
Willing him to the impossible,
we clapped till he hurled all seven shiny bats
into an undetected pattern,
then we roared with approval;
one of us had beaten the odds.

Performers all, we arrange and order,
text and tumble,
run to people and places chasing our purposes and goals.
Like funambulists we try not to fall.

Meanwhile at the circus,
beauties balanced on the rims of giant hoops
circling slow around the stage,
their legs full of secret strength,
while an ebony haired enchantress
sang a haunting, deep song
calling out creatures from the mist and myths of Mexico.
Silently these beings appeared,
dressed in suits and skirts,
with masks of zebras, crocodiles and birds,
and it made me cry
because all people really want is to be happy at the circus,
waving to the crowd, parading around fanciful and fine
as someone sings an ageless song,
girls jump and are caught by strong, careful men.

Last Autumn

Perhaps
this will be all that remains of the world
after the final war,
the final pestilence and the final
shout from the crowd.
Perhaps this will be all anyone finds
in the ruin and the rubble
of what was once such a prized and positioned nation;
this little message,
retrieved from a blue and silver flash drive.

It will say that all September and into October,
I kept looking and wondering at the signs around me,
feeling like it could be the last autumn,
because you were leaving home.

It would be a grand adventure
taking you away to drink with foreign men,
dance with beautiful girls,
and my message will say
it felt like it could be the last autumn
because you told me you loved me
though you had to go.

The afternoon you readied to leave we stood together,
surrounded by people who never really knew us.
You made me look into your soft, dark eyes
and you said,
"There will be other summers."

But this could be
the last autumn.

Golden Cloud

A golden cloud of leaves falls
outside my window as I sit in bed—
front row seat to the change.

It is the fall, when
Nature shows its power and fragility
all at once,
shouts before being suborned
by that colder, stronger force;
 a little death can do that.

But now, as the gold bursts through the green
before being mottled and ruined in the damp,
it claims its beauteous victory,
a light in all eyes that can see.

Sunflower

I want a sunflower.

Big, filling both hands,
heavy-headed, dusting me with pollen,
with blooming dreams.

Big enough to fill senses,
block discouragement,
yellow petal blades and sienna-earth eye
the only things in view.

A platter of beauty serving up hope,
prosperity, happiness,
impressions of love.

I want a sunflower.

Demanding in its existence,
a startling presence in the room,
laying face up, too large for a vase,
claiming the table's center for its home;
a county-fair blue ribbon winner,
statement of glory,
speaking only of only the possible.

I want a sunflower.

Wiser

The hot hand of the sun
touched my arm and I knew
solitude was a good thing--
 a desirable thing; as desirable
as the man I once loved or
the jewel I once bought after
saving money for a long time.

Walking,
grasses, weeds and giant ferns
popped out,
proof
that spring had indeed overcome
the harsh hardship of winter
where a month earlier
only muck, detritus and previous leaves
refused hope along the road.

Ah, this road.
Walked by me
twenty years now,
and I can say
I am wiser.

Karen Warinsky was able to get back to pleasure writing once her now grown children were older. On a whim she entered a poem in the 2011 Montreal International Poetry Contest where her piece, "Roodhouse" was long-listed. Two years later she was named a finalist in the same contest, and those top 50 entries were published in an anthology by Véhicule Press.

Since then she has published several pieces including a memoir about her grandmother in the book *Dear Nana*, two poems in the recent release *Nuclear Impact: Broken Atoms in Our Hands*, a poem in the February 2018 edition of *Blue Heron,* and works in 2017 and 2018 editions of *Light; a Journal of Photography and Poetry*, based in New York City.

Warinsky, a native of Illinois, has lived in North Dakota, Washington State, Japan, and has resided in Connecticut since 1988. Her topics range from connecting nature to the divine, motherhood, and mid-life and her tone covers the spectrum from the ironic to the awestruck. She has worked in public relations, radio, television and print media and taught English for 20 years. She holds a BS in Journalism from Northern Illinois University and she has a Master of Arts in English from Fitchburg State University.

Contact her on Twitter @KWarinsky

Karen Warinsky's Gold in Autumn is a book of just the sort of poetry the world needs right now; it's a poetry concerned above all with the beauties of life. Nor does Warinsky shy away from considerations of mortality which serve to augment that beauty with the riskiest of sentiments in our times: nostalgia. In an age swept up with activism and shrill political poetry on the one hand and sterile observation on the other, this book offers a refuge and antidote by giving the heart-life a primary place in the scheme of human priorities. This is a poetry that, to borrow one of Warinsky's analogies, is "not smooth, cool granite where a daily dust / of troubles / can be wiped away." This poetry is "craggy," and full of feeling, "catching all the errors of love."
    --Asa Boxer, Founder and Manager of the Montreal International Poetry Prize; editor of *The Secular Heretic*

****

Karen Warinsky's new poetry collection is *A platter of beauty serving up hope* --- the inescapable bond between all living things is *a solid... cold stone [that] seems to satisfy* our lowest lows... the agonizing nostalgia of being alone. We are *refugees roaming the world* eagerly in search of opportunities to escape into divine expressions; *we rise... we sing.*
--Michal Mahgerefteh, Editor-in-Chief, *Mizmor Anthology*

****

Karen Warinsky's poetry employs images that are at once concrete and yet ethereal enough to evoke a myriad of emotional responses from her reader. From her masterful evocation of aging, to her gripping character study and social commentary in "Tough Girls," Warinsky's particular gift shines forth in her ability to take her reader on a spiritual journey from the mundane to the sublime.
--Matthew J. Carr, director, Pilgrim Soul Productions